ME, MYSELF,
AND PARKINSON'S

ME, MYSELF, AND PARKINSON'S

GEORGE TAIT JR.

PARTRIDGE

To order additional copies of this book, contact
Toll Free 800 101 2657 (Singapore)
Toll Free 1 800 81 7340 (Malaysia)
orders.singapore@partridgepublishing.com

www.partridgepublishing.com/singapore

Parkinson's Disease – 4 years in the life of…..

1 APR – IT ALL STARTED WHEN....

APRIL 1, 2015

It was sometime in July 2011 when i awoke in the middle of the night feeling cramping pains in my lower right arm.

I initially thought nothing of it, thinking that perhaps it was the result of some over-strenuous activity from the gym a few days before. The pain however, persisted and about 4 days later i noticed that my right thumb began to tremble mildly. The cramping pain & trembling continued for a few more days and i then decided that "Google" would be the source of my self-diagnosis.

Hmm, ***"BET (Benign Essential Tremor)"*** & ***"PD (Parkinson's Disease)"*** were the two most likely causes I 'Googley' concluded, ultimately convincing myself that "Essential Tremor" was the more likely culprit, with me being "just" 50 years young and in an otherwise relatively healthy state. And so it was with renewed self assuredness that i went on with life until...

2 APR – THE TRUTH HURTS...

APRIL 2, 2015

...the pain and tremors persisted to the extent that i had begun to doubt my own conclusion. I then made an appointment to see a neurologist at Damansara Specialist Hospital (DSH), it being the most conveniently located hospital in relation to my then residential address.

On the day of the appointment i sauntered into the neuro's office still mildly confident that my ailment was no more than BET. The neuro (a young slightly brash individual), proceeded to put me through some physical tests (after viewing the tremors in my thumb) and concluded that it was probably a harmless form of BET and advised that should the tremors persist and subsequently worsen in a couple of months, to pay him a return visit with no medication prescribed to treat the tremors nor the cramping pain in my lower right arm. Hey, i could have saved myself some $$$ i thought and happy in the knowledge that all was well....

All was however not well, as in a space of 2 months the tremors had spread to my right fist n palm and the pain persisted, after which time i thought that something more serious was behind the tremors and cramping pains. I decided not to return to the 1st neuro (for reasons unknown or perhaps his lack of bedside manners) and did some checking for neuros specialising in Movement Disorders specifically PD (now was the time the worrying and paranoia had started, and it wasn't funny...). I decided on Dr MK Lee at Pantai Medical Centre (PMC), a middle aged lady with a calm if somewhat intimidating nature (Prim and proper with immaculate English which reminded me of an

Chemistry Lecturer during my college days, her name i forget now) which i subsequently came to be comfortable with and appreciated. So on the day of the appointment it was with blurriness and gnawing fear that i met Dr Lee and she put me through the same physical tests that the DSH neuro had put me through. "So, she says, calmly, it looks likely that you have early stage PD for which there are no chemical tests to confirm this diagnosis". "Take the meds that i shall be giving you today and if the pain and tremors recede, then it is confirmed that you have PD" she says, still her calmness the prevailing and only comforting emotion that i could cling to....

With that somewhat assured manner in which she drew her conclusions and diagnosis, I recall vividly trudging out of her office in a state of confusion, worry and sadness, the latter being the most overwhelming emotion. It would be a week later that i returned to see the good doctor and ......

3 APR – FFWD 2015 – A DIGRESSION, THE PRODIGAL SON.

APRIL 3, 2015

It was 15 March 2015 when I got the news that my dad had suffered a massive stroke. He was hospitalised and passed away on 25 March 2015.

This year has been particularly difficult due to unexpected progression of my PD to a Stage that has even my Bangkok neuro baffled. That coupled with the death of my father whom i had sought solace in every time the latest effects from PD hit me, just was a despairing period for me. It is the support that i receive from friends and family that has kept me sane till today. I try to remain happy and optimistic as is possible and the conception of this blog has been therapeutic for me. It is hoped that it is in this spirit that my blog is read and not as an exercise in narcissism by me.

Being a George and the only male child in the family was not fun especially during the late teenage years when Academic achievement seemed the paramount and only objective in life. With all the high hopes and expectations of sending your child to a further overseas education it was much shame and disappointment that must have enveloped my father when his only son came home with nought. It was to be almost a year before he could muster a complete sentence to convey to me. I understood his reasons and was grateful that he had come to terms with my abject failure.

And so the wounds would, over time, heal. And it was after his retirement from the Police Force that he would transform into the man whom i shall remember, always. Being a senior cop brings with it the authoritative, no-nonsense, forceful, i'm-always-right persona and it is with much love and affection that i shower him with credit, praise and admiration that he was the man he was, who gave me everything within his means, both materially and emotionally, till his dying day. I remember the times (and there were many) when the PD was so crippling that i would call him just to hear his comforting voice and all the morose thoughts and feelings abated. I miss you dad, and may your soul forever rest in peace. With love, your son.

6 APR – AND SO YOUR WORLD STARTS A CRUMBLING…..

APRIL 6, 2015

.and so i step into Dr Lee's room and she begins asking slowly, " So, Mr Tait, How do you feel ?" I hesitantly reply, " I think so, Doc, the cramps have definitely gone and the tremors are about 90 percent down from before, what does it mean ?" She coolly replies, "I think it is quite certain that you have PD but unfortunately there are no tests to confirm this a 100 percent ." With those words still ringing in my ears, i can barely remember what happened next, save finding myself sitting in front of my pc researching the effects of PD, which did not make for pleasant reading….

I remember tears rolling down my cheeks as i began to digest the words on the computer screen :

Parkinson's "non-motor "symptoms

Dementia & Alzheimer's, Cognitive impairment – In most cases, Alzheimer's & dementia in Parkinson's occurs late in the disease, as the pathology starts to spread outside of the motor areas and into cognitive areas.

Depression and anxiety – Depression can be an early sign of the disease. Living with Parkinson's can certainly cause stress and sadness, depression may also be caused by changes in areas of the brain that affect mood. Anxiety often occurs with depression in Parkinson's. As with depression, anxiety can be an early sign of Parkinson's.

Hallucinations – In Parkinson's, hallucinations are almost always visual (you see something that is not there). They commonly begin as minor, non-threatening visual images. At first, most people are aware that the hallucinations are not real. Later on, what is real may become blurred.

Sexual dysfunction – The risk of aberrant sexual behaviour such as hypersexuality, exhibitionism, or pederasty occur in Parkinson's disease. Patients should be aware of increased sexual impulses or reduced behavioural control and hypersexuality and sexually deviant behaviour in Parkinson's disease and dopaminergic therapy.

Delusions – are false beliefs that are not based on reality or fact. Delusions may occur after having hallucinations. Suspicions are most often directed at family members. Common delusions include cheating spouses or theft. Delusions mainly occur in advanced Parkinson's.

REM sleep behaviour disorder -REM (rapid eye movement) sleep is one of the five stages of sleep. Normally, there is no movement during REM sleep (you are paralyzed). If you have REM sleep behaviour disorder (RBD), this normal paralysis is lost. RBD may cause you to act out your dreams. You may punch, kick, shout, talk or fall out of bed during this stage. You may end up injuring yourself or your bed partner.

Parkinson's "motor "symptoms :

Resting Tremor – In the early stages of the disease, about 70 percent of people experience a slight tremor in the hand or foot on one side of the body, or less commonly in the jaw or face.

Bradykinesia – Bradykinesia means "slow movement." A defining feature of Parkinson's, bradykinesia also describes a general reduction of spontaneous movement, which can give the appearance of abnormal stillness and a decrease in facial expressivity. Due to bradykinesia, a person with Parkinson's may have difficulty performing everyday functions,such as buttoning a shirt, cutting food or brushing his or her teeth. Bradykinesia can affect a person's speech, which may become quieter and less distinct as Parkinson's progresses.

Rigidity – Rigidity causes stiffness and inflexibility of the limbs, neck and trunk contributing to a decreased range of motion.

Postural Instability – One of the most important signs of Parkinson's is postural instability, a tendency to be unstable when standing upright. A person with postural instability may topple backwards if jostled even slightly. Some develop a dangerous tendency to sway backwards when rising from a chair, standing or turning. Many people with Parkinson's are unable to recover, and would tumble backwards if someone were not right there to catch him or her.

Freezing – Freezing of gait is an important sign of PD. People who experience freezing will normally hesitate before stepping forward. They feel as if their feet are glued to the floor. Freezing can occur in very specific situations, such as when starting to walk, when pivoting, when crossing a threshold or doorway, and when approaching a chair. Freezing is a potentially serious problem in Parkinson's disease, as it may increase a person's risk of falling forward.

Micrographia – This term is the name for a shrinkage in handwriting that progresses the more a person with Parkinson's writes, eventually resulting in his total inability to write.

It was months of depression, suicidal thoughts and reexamination of faith that followed, until i then made a life changing decision to….

http://www.pdf.org/symptoms_primary
http://www.pdf.org/symptoms_secondary

An aside:

Writing my blog has been an experience, with encouraging words from family and friends that help to sustain the drive to document what i need to before it becomes a physical impossibility. The difficult part about documenting my struggle coping with PD is trying continually, to maintain the faithfulness to the the memories, facts and events whilst ensuring that the honesty and frankness of what is written doesn't hurt family n friends in the process. I sincerely hope that what i've written hasn't caused nor will cause in the future any irreparable pain….Thank you.

6 APR 2 – CHAOS, ACRIMONY, BITTERNESS, RESOLUTION...

<u>APRIL 6, 2015</u>

....I had been working for a local Financial Institution (FI aka bank) since December 1984 without much drama nor major issues, as the FI then was under the helm of Malaysians who to our credit, at least possess a modicum of conscience. I had gone through many, many bosses by then and all had contributed to my growth and progression through the ranks until my last designation as AVP, Payment Centre, Treasury Ops. It was when the most influential position (CXX) within the FI was relinquished to a person of kiasu inclinations that things began to change for the worse.

Cost cutting, entity reorganisation, staff redeployment, KPIs, performance assessments were taken to "new heights" which could only lead to one obvious conclusion, the staff reduction and hence mutual separation exercise. With my need for constant medical treatment and day offs and hence the accompanying costs, it was obvious that i would be on the wanted list. It was not a pleasant new working environment that was developing when your new immediate boss on a daily basis pops in to your department and area of expertise to strut her new found power and conduct inane and asinine checks on staff performance with unwarranted cruel comments thrown in for good measure. To cut a long story short the battle ended with me receiving a mutually agreed separation scheme and some financial compensation. It was some months later that i heard that the ex-immediate boss's husband had suddenly passed away, recalling gleefully (at that time, which i now regret and apologize for) that she had finally received her karma. It was early 2012 when i left the organization i had worked in for the last 28 years of my life and had arrived at the crossroads of the rest of my life.....

7 APR 1 – THE ONLY CONSTANT IN LIFE…

<u>APRIL 8, 2015</u>

…The months that followed were spent reassessing the priorities in my life, forecasting both the financial and emotional costs, subjecting myself to a trial of drug acclimatization with a cocktail of drugs : Selegiline aka Jumex, Sifrol, Amantadine, Trivastal, Memantine and Azilect.

The side effects from some of the meds that i consumed were so severe that i had to discontinue taking them, some with "milder" side effects, that i just had to live with. Trivastal Retard was one drug in particular that was commonly prescribed to PD patients that i just could not tolerate. I remember taking it for the first time and had such extreme suicidal thoughts that i ended up crying continuously for 5 hours after nearly hurling myself off my 18th floor balcony. The consumption of this drug in particular, was a result of "too many cooks" as I had been seeing a number of neuros by then and making a guinea pig of myself with the juggling of their recommended drugs. With the unpleasant reaction to Trivastal, i decided to then narrow down my "cooks" to just Dr MK Lee of PMC and Dr Oraporn of Bumrungrad Hospital which has worked till today. Both docs have different approaches to treating PD & both are excellent doctors in my eyes…

Then came the difficult decision on what i wanted to do for the rest of my life.The overwhelming emotion i had felt and still feel, since the diagnosis was one that, i wanted / needed to do and experience things in my life that i hadn't and within the time frame of what's left of the number of years before my mind and body give up on me. What i finally determined to be best for me would have undoubtedly hurt those closest to me and for that i apologize sincerely and hope that over time, they come to understand my actions which will be construed by some as selfish, self- centered /serving /indulgent and narcissistic...

7 Apr 2 – Going back to my roots...

APRIL 8, 2015

... i have two kids, one, 27 years old and the other, 22. My wife and i, have both provided for them with what i believe was more than adequate. The eldest, Keisha, is a Mass Comm. Grad., and my son Aeyden, is a soon to be an IT Grad. Both were provided with enough pocket money and a car each for college commute and daily use.I was the "bad cop", the one always on their case, the one constantly nagging at them and the one constantly barking out instructions at them. I know that it must have seemed to them, like they had this crazed man living with them. I make no apologies for my behavior then as i know first hand what it is like to screw up an academic opportunity and living with the regret. I hope they understand the reasons for my actions and that my intentions were good.With the self belief / knowledge that i had done what was expected of me as a parent and husband, at least in my eyes, i decided to break the news of my next step in life.

My wife Ursula and i had over the years spent many holidays in Thailand, especially Bangkok. It is for us a special country, a place where the people are friendly, the weather is nice, the food is great and where the cost of living is lower than KL. If one is not gullible nor naive, you will truly get value for money in terms of your purchases in goods and services. More often than not, you will not feel ripped off after paying for a meal as the prices are low for the quality of food you receive. The Soi parallel to the one I'm living on in Bangkok sells food, fruits, vegetables, spices, deserts, pharmaceutical drugs, t-shirts, electronic gadgets etc at unbeatable prices. A kg of Chiangmai strawberries cost just THB 120 and a delicious meal of fei-chee-yoke or tau-eu-bak with rice, salted vege and hard boiled egg where the portions of rice and tau-eu-bak are more than enough for two, costs just THB 60. Thai and aromatic massage costs just THB 30 per hour and the maintenance fee i pay for my condo entitles me to staff maintenance services up midnight daily. Alcoholic beverages are affordable too and taxi rides half KL prices (if one is willing to sit through traffic).

Personal safety and security is another like and...

9 APR – A BAD DAY AT THE OFFICE…

APRIL 8, 2015

…for much of the last 4 years since i have been diagnosed with PD, i have had the following PD related symptoms :

Symptom	Emo Scale
• inability to write and sign my name	2
• soft, stammered, fast and often incoherent speech	4
• delusions	4
• urinary incontinence	3
• tremors on the whole right arm	3
• depression and anxiety	4
• nightly sleep talking, REM sleep behaviour disorder	2
• rigidity	4
• extreme daytime sleepiness & tiredness	3
• excessive salivating	2
• dry eyes	1
• nightly cramping in both legs	3
• freezing	5
• postural instability	5

Emo Scale:

1 – Irritating

2 – Tolerable

3 – Tolerable but slightly depressing

4 – Depressing with negative thoughts

5 – Totally fucked up

I feel the need to document today's post when it is still fresh in my mind for the benefit of my own sanity as perhaps it would reinforce mentally the need for me to be vigilant at all times and process the mechanics of my next attempted physical forward motion.

It was in October of last year, in Seoul, Korea that i had my first fall. I was facing the mirror in the hotel bathroom and attempting to turn around and exit the bathroom when as my upper torso turned in anticipation of my feet shuffling in the next sequence of movement, my feet froze and i fell heavily onto my side just narrowly avoiding the toilet bowl and partly breaking my fall with my right forearm. I remember screaming out in frustration and pain as my forearm and the right side of my upper torso hit the bathroom floor. No one came to my aid as i lay there in pain thinking, "wtf !! why didn't i just break my effing skull and just effing die !!" The next 4 days were spent in my hotel room recovering from the pain and bruising from the heavy fall and hoping that i'd be able to make my scheduled flight back to Bangkok. I did not see a doctor as i did not take up travel / medical insurance (a stupid thing to not do) and anticipated that the bill would be a killer to my budget.

The falls would come more frequently (around 7 falls in the space of 2 months) causing varied degrees of pain and embarrassment before i finally decided to pay a visit to Dr Oraporn. Also an increase in dosage of Sifrol as I had already maxxed out my Jumex, amantadine and had stopped Azilect due to the prohibitive cost relative to its benefits. And so the frequency of the falls decreased if i remembered to take them on time. And then, it was yesterday night after arriving home from dinner and attempting to exit my car in the car park when i lost all feeling in my left leg and nearly fell over. After about 20 minutes of siting in my car, the feeling returned to my left leg after which i subsequently lugged myself into my room. The rest of the last night and this morning the feeling of frozen feet was so prevalent in spite of having taken my meds on time. Then familiar feeling of shittiness and depression took over. At around 12 pm in the afternoon, (the normal time for my 1st dose of meds) i took double the dosage of memantine, 20 mg (my daily max) instead of the usual 10 mg and it seems to be working so far. However, as i have already maxxed out my memantine for the day, i will have to skip it at my next dose at midnight tonight and see what happens tomorrow...

10 APR – And life 'should' go on…

APRIL 10, 2015

…i usually get up to go to the loo about 5 times a night. As I attempt to get up from bed, i need the "walker" with a 4 pronged base as support so i can "push" myself up from bed (if that makes any sense) as both my feet feel "dead". And then the challenge begins when on successfully getting up, both feet "freeze" when you attempt to take your first steps. So without the "walker" i would definitely fall over. This has been happening more frequently and there used to be good nights and bad nights but now there are only bad nights.….

The trip to ease my bladder can be pretty hazardous, with my all glass sliding door in the way (to keep the cool air from my room a/c from "escaping"), Scotty also will spread himself across the hallway like a little scarecrow waiting to be tread on and a small glass topped dinner table beside the door to the loo (yes, the condo is that small) completes the obstacle course. So far, I've made it to & from the loo nightly without mishap but how long my luck holds out is the question (Yes, i know an alternative solution, but it does not make for pleasant reading nor sleeping). So it was biz as usual last night, until i got up around 9 am this morning and with the "frozen feet" feeling still with me. And so with laptop on er, my lap and laying in bed, i booked a ticket online to catch "Fast & Furious 7" at the IMAX at EMQuartier, Phrom Phong. The next couple of hours were spent just lazing around in bed (with occasional forays into the kitchen) trying to stay safe. The "frozen feet" thawed to a satisfactory degree and I opted for a cab to take me to the cineplex just in case and had a pretty good day at the movies....(F & F 7 in 3D is pretty amazing).

I truly hope that all days will be like today but unfortunately it's only a matter of time before the bubble bursts...So the battle goes on and i can only try to make the rest of my life, the best of my life

11 APR – PIGGING OUT & A
GOOD BUDDY VISITS…

APRIL 11, 2015

…Today has been a good day, tremors were only obvious when eating, the depressions non intrusive and the "Freezing" and Postural instability manageable. And so i decided to do something out of sheer gluttony and also just because i was still on a high from yesterday's serenity (from the PD point of view).

I had on 2 occasions driven from On Nut to Mo Chit and back (total approx 60 km) for the registration and checking of 2 vehicles purchased, by the Thai RTD. Lunch on both occasions was at this nondescript little "cafe" that served Thai dishes which i had stumbled upon whilst driving around the Mo Chit and Saphan Khwai BTS stations. The food at this joint was so tasty and cheap and the portions generous.

It was around 11.30 am and with my tummy starting to growl, that i got into my car and sped to this cafe (the name of which i forget).On arrival, i ordered Tom Yum Goong, Phad Kra Pao Moo (pork) and squid fried with salted egg (which was my super favorite dish) and plain white rice. I demolished said meal in record time and departed said premises feeling like a pig, but what a totally satisfying meal it was, which cost me a meager THB 250. On the way home, I popped by Tesco's to replenish my groceries stock as a good buddy of mine would be visiting me from KL and arriving at Suvarnabhumi in a few hours time. BK Tan has been a good friend, one who has listened to my constant life, tearful depressive stage mutterings and other "fuck the world" moanings with calmness, objectivity, clarity and unwavering patience. I drove to Suvarnabhumi airport to pick him up and we were back in my condo around 6 pm and planning our activities for the night…

Just a cautionary note :

My fellow PD sufferers on similar meds as i, please err on the side of caution and attempt long drives only after you've pumped a few cups of caffeine rich coffee into your system (and on a day when your tremors are down in intensity), because extreme sleepiness will devour your attention span & result in an untoward incident & the LAW biting your ass off.

12 APR – A GOOD BUDDY VISITS, PART 2…

…The previous nite was spent at Mojo's, an Aussie owned restaurant & bar in soi 33, Sukhumvit road. BK Tan and I spent a few hours there just playing pool (THB 30 per game), listening to a Filipino Band playing good live music, having a few drinks and coyote gawking.

The next morning, we got up bright and early and headed for the Erawan Museum which is on the outskirts of the city. You can take the eastbound BTS (skytrain) (the extension of the BTS, currently under construction, will take you very close to Erawan Museum), currently the last station is Bearing from which you need to take a cab (THB 60-70). We drove which took us about 35 minutes in light traffic, it being the eve of Songkran Festival, with most BKK inhabitants having left for their hometowns already. It is a lovely and serene place to spend a couple of hours contemplating and praying to the lord Buddha. It is magnificently well maintained and definitely well worth a visit.

After the Erawan Museum, we made our way to Mega Banga, my favorite Mall in Bangkok as it has a huge selection of stores, and it isn't as crowded as most of the other malls.They provide a free bus service to and from the Udom Suk BTS station, so getting there is really easy. They have IKEA, Robinsons, Uniqlo, Living Index, a cinema and a wide selection of restaurants esp. my fav chinese restaurant, The Four Seasons. Fantastic pork dishes and vegetables at slightly dearer price than other similar restaurants but you get chinese food at its best, i feel. The rest of the day after MB was spent just chilling n watching TV after which we grabbed an early night's sleep.

13 APR – CAN'T LIVE WITH THEM, CAN'T LIVE WITHOUT THEM...

APRIL 15, 2015

...Today, Monday the 13th, is the first day of Songkran, the traditional Thai new year. The Songkran festival falls in mid-April every year and it is the most important event of the year for the Thai people.The traditional water pouring is meant as a symbol of washing away all of one's sins and is sometimes filled with fragrant herbs when celebrated in the traditional manner. However, nowadays the celebration is normally marked by the spraying of water at one another with any equipment at one's disposal at that time. it has become a favorite practice that hordes of kids, teenagers and even (or rather especially) adults now fully equip themselves with the latest water guns / cannons waiting to unleash a hail of water splashes and sprays at anyone who walks by.

To think of writing on my blog seemed like a task too far what with my daily chores of feeding and picking up after Scotty, laundry n sweeping my condo unit. By the time i recovered, it was pretty much evening and BK Tan and I headed to MIXX Club at President Tower, Ploen Chit. The club is an ok place to hang out as it has two sections playing different genres of music but it gets bad publicity because certain nationalities are denied entry. It was a quite quiet, we had a few beers, listened to some house n R & B and then went home, me still feeling stoned...

16 APR – Shitty day

APRIL 16, 2015

God, i swear, if i get a few more shit ass days like this, i'll just bloody end it all…

18 APR – I WRITE WHAT I WRITE...

APRIL 17, 2015

...Dear readers, I sincerely apologize for my previous post. It has been a tough few days for me, the tiredness having reached a level that was difficult to handle and comprehend. It was especially bad on 16 APR when all i felt was this overwhelming tiredness and depression taking over body, mind and soul.

All i wanted to do was to not have to think or deliberate on the multitude of thoughts that were going through my mind. And i could only hear myself saying over and over "give up, give up, it's time to leave this shitty world behind",contemplating on what was the easiest route to achieve that. objective. I know i'm supposed to, thru my blog, also attempt to be a source of encouragement for fellow PD sufferers but it's fucking hard work.

I hope that from now (4 am on 18 APR), i shall succeed in my endeavour to be stronger and not let PD beat the crap out of me...

20 APR – Feeling better…

APRIL 20, 2015

It's really had a positive effect on my mobility and balance. The problem of the difficulty in getting up from a sitting position and initiating the subsequent forward movement or steps seem to have improved by at least 80 percent. I feel so much more confident getting up to go to the loo at night. It's worked wonders for my psyche.

It was 3 days ago that a Thai friend asked me if I'd be interested to join her in a small business venture. She had managed to secure a store around my condo area roughly about 120 sq ft in size and with a daily rental rate of THB 800. She mentioned that we could operate a ladies apparel shop selling all sorts of ladies garments like denim shorts, skirts, dresses, ladies Ts, blouses etc. Since i needed a boost in my life to help me forget a little about my PD, i decided to join her. And so it's been an exciting 3 days for me getting up at 4 a.m. and going down to the market to pick n choose the designs of garments that we think would be popular and also setting up the store in terms of appeal and attractiveness to walk in customers.

I have also suggested to my partner that we'd try to sell the items online also and as such would like to post on my blog under the My Pics section a few of the items that we have available for order. The prices are in THB and are excl. delivery charges. I hope that you guys like some of the items and feel free to place your orders. Items ordered in bulk (10 or more per item) will be discounted THB 20. Thank you.

22 APR – Hmm...

APRIL 22, 2015

...Today's been a so-so kind of day. Just that the tiredness seems to be creeping back in along with the freezing and postural instability. I'm going to try something that was suggested by friends through a YouTube video regarding the positive effects of cycling on Parkinson's patients.

I will try to get a gym bike and attempt some sort of fitness and cycling programme that has been known to work for PD patients. Will keep my fellow PD sufferers updated ...

23 APR – INSOMNIAC ALIVE...

APRIL 22, 2015

...Like some crazy ass dude listening to my music @ 4 am, since i just can't sleep...Tried to order a sausage Mcmuffin b'fast set and the operator says that i should only start ordering at 5 am...then why the fxxk would he even bother answering the call ??!! You'd thought McD's would have in place some tele-answering machine for "outside biz hours" calls. Anyways ended up eating 2 peanut butter sandwiches downed with 2 cups of Moccona coffee @ 3.45 am. What happened to the grandiose exercise plans pray tell ? It's still very much on my mind, just need to remain focussed and keep improving my fitness level to a level that, well, i hope, makes the PD more tolerable...

So with Lisa Stansfield belting out over my earphones one of the best pop tunes of all time " i've been around the world", i sit in front of my PC wondering if i would have the drive or energy to see my upcoming project through to fruition. There is this cool little cafe on Sukhumvit Soi 50 called 'Ooh la la' which serves one of many delicious b'fast sets – Poached eggs with salmon, sausage, eggs & bacon, ham and croissant served with a good selection of local & imported coffees. The lunch menu isn't too bad either with dishes like "Spicy cowgirl", "Sweet home the Link" and "Khaw Phad ham with miso soup". I've been eyeing the franchise for this cafe for some time now and decided to approach the owner...

25 APR – NEVER THE SAME AGAIN…PART 1…

APRIL 27, 2015

…I receive a call yesterday morning and the male caller says " Hi, Is this George ? I'm X, the son of Mr & Mrs. Y, who are old friends of your parents. I am in Thailand for a few days and your mum asked me to find out if you're ok, whether you are able to handle yourself in Bangkok and whether you need any sort of help ?" And he further went on to mention that I could contact him if I needed any assistance, all the time sounding really worried and concerned.

I am really grateful and thankful that a stranger (to me) was willing to provide unconditional assistance and that's also down to our mutual parents' relationship and don't get me wrong, again, I say, I'm truly grateful, but what I don't need at this stage in the disease is charity or pity, just understanding from family and friends that no matter how much I wish things to be the same, they never will be again.

It's been difficult for some, I know, when I used to lose my temper over the smallest issue, when I get obsessively crazy and become paranoid or delusional or when I'd spend hours keeping you awake by my sleep talking and dream re-enactments and my accusations and insinuations and those "non-motor" symptoms together with the movement disorder ones which required attention must be and have been, so draining…I offer no excuses, just appeal for understanding that I am really **NOT** the person with all the above-mentioned traits and that it's been a daily struggle for me both emotionally and physically ever since God bestowed PD on me. (And to my closest buddies, who I know, must sometimes be so fed up of my whinings, thank you for your unwavering support.)

To my fellow PD sufferers, any feedback on this post would be appreciated…

27 APR – NEVER THE SAME AGAIN ...PART 2...

... I remember the fonder memories from times gone by, like sitting at the dinner table in my grandma's house in Rangoon road, Penang, when she'd prepare a lunch meal of fried fish mixed with thick black sauce and sugar and this would then be hand kneaded into a serving of white rice and hand fed to me. I must have been 5 or 6 years old at that time. I can still taste this meal on the days when melancholy sets in and all you would wish for was for the simpler(childhood) days of innocence and where the future seemed so,so far away...She was the epitome of cool, never seemed to get angry nor upset but maintaining the aura of authority and always the matriarch of the Tait clan, since my granddad had passed away a few years before (when I was 3 years old, I believe). My relationship with my grandma was a special one, and she was the one person in my life that personified the magical, kind, considerate, loving and unadulterated human characteristics that we all strived to attain, once, a long time ago. Whenever my parents headed up to Penang during the December school holidays when I was younger, I'd spend nights at grandma's and I would sleep in the same bed as her and I remember her waking me up a few times during the night to visit the loo (yes urinary problems even back then). When she passed away it was a sad day and I was in fifth form at the time, and I remember arriving late at night at Rangoon road and walking up her coffin and bawling my eyes out when I saw her...On some nights, I see her in my dreams and she is sitting down in that familiar chair and she says "It's ok, ah Jot, I will always be here ..."

to be continued...

31

29 APR – NEVER THE SAME AGAIN...PART 3...

APRIL 29, 2015

...FFWD 1988... My beautiful girl, Keisha, was born on 20 September, and to witness her birth was an amazing experience. I remember the doctor telling my wife, "Push !, Push !" and then seeing the top of my baby's head with her dark hair appear and then as if with some unreal speed, the next scene had changed to the doctor lifting her up on "expulsion" and saying "Congrats, you have a beautiful baby girl !". She was indeed beautiful, arriving seemingly as 6 month old with her generous crown of dark brown hair, well formed body and a cherubic face.

And so the next 22 years would pan out as I had planned for her, from the sleepless nights of nappy changing, the frequent check ups to the doctors, the Father-daughter holidays together when she was around 3 years old to visit my parents in Penang, the first day at nursery school when she looked super cute in her "uniform", the primary, secondary school, and College days when the "bad cop" persona emerged and she was then "indoctrinated" with the same mind set that I encountered during my teenage years (with differing results), that education was EVERYTHING. Perhaps the execution lacked finesse but my intentions were good. Then came the day that was one of the happiest in my life, when she went up to the podium to collect her BA Degree scroll and I felt like my life had been a journey fulfilled...And ever since, she has blossomed into the individual that I had hoped she'd be, to be as independent a woman that she could be, both financially and emotionally and to be subservient to no man.

I hope that she will look back at those days when her father was crazily tyrannical and comprehend and realize that I did what I did because of my love for her. She is and always will be the one true love of my life…

9 May – Life's a lady, and then you die…

…I never had the articulation of speech, more so in front a crowd. However with the progression of PD, I can't even string a proper sentence together nowadays without my attempted speech sounding soft, unclear, mumbled, stammered and as if at the speed of light. So to a person whom say, I've just met, and who is at the other end listening, he/she must think that I'm a moron. …

The people who come in contact with me often, have somehow developed the ability to decipher the message I'm trying to convey, but to others it must be painfully annoying trying to engage in conversation with me. Even the wife doesn't understand what the fuck I'm saying sometimes…It's become such a fucking chore and embarrassment to speak, these past few months, and I know that it will only get worse. My BKK doc has recommended that i go for speech therapy, but i think that just keeping my mouth shut would be a cheaper option.

And then the falls return…it was the day the wife was returning to KL on 3 May, that on retrieving my plastic tumbler of cold water from the fridge and taking the next step forward that my right foot just froze as if it had lost all feeling and I fell forward towards the kitchen floor. I instinctively threw the tumbler as far away for me as I possibly could and hit the floor with both arms breaking my fall with the palms and elbows sorely bruised. And so it has been a week when even getting up from bed or a chair has been so difficult and with the falls just waiting to register a break or crack in some part of my anatomy that also came the realization that my driving ability has now become shit. On making a U-turn, I am unable to steer the car back into a directly forward trajectory quickly enough and so almost ended up ploughing into the culvert, divider or a car on several occasions.

The faltering speech together with the postural instability and 'freezing' episodes which have returned to bite my ass with a vengeance, and the rapid deterioration of my driving skills have on writing this post, made this a quite miserable endeavour. So with that, my day comes to an end and may tomorrow bring sunshine and the promise of better things so that I may see the reasons why life is worth, well, ...

10 May – Of driving and mad drivers…

There is an accepted code of driving behavior in Bangkok (and other parts of Thailand), where if a driver indicates his intention to lane change by using his signal lights and no matter how last minute his lane change actions are, the other drivers would accept it and allow the said driver to change lanes or encroach into their lanes. Having driven from Bangkok to Chonburi & Pattaya regularly and also to Koh Chang and Hua Hin over my 1 1/2 years in Thailand, it would seem that my assumption of the existence of such a code is true.

Having loved to drive since a young age, it was with much sadness that I recently realized that with a progressive degenerative disease like PD, once the meds fail to stem the deterioration of whatever physical attributes or agility you might have possessed, it's time to seriously consider alternative solutions. A recent incident which could have or could not have been my fault, sort of made my mind up for me that I would not put another person's life or my own in harms way if there was an alternative solution. So I have decided that effective today I would only use the BTS or Grab Taxi to get around and use the car only in the event of an emergency.

What happened about a week ago was when after meeting up with a friend from Malaysia at Central World in Phloen Chit – Prattunam, I wrongly exited from the mall into Rajadamri Road instead of Phloen Chit – Sukhumvit. Realizing that I had to quickly proceed to the traffic lights which lead to Petchburi Road via the extreme right lane and hence my alternative route home, I signaled my intention to switch lanes and on seeing that the lane was clear, then moved over 2 lanes and on my approach to the final right lane saw this humongous tourist bus that must have been at least 7 to 8 feet behind and so I continued with my lane change. On seeing that I was going to move into his lane, the driver accelerated his vehicle until it was almost at my tail. I then accelerated too otherwise I would miss my right turn into Petchburi Road at the traffic light junction. And so began this short drag race to the traffic light junction with this mother fucker coming so close to my ass and attempting to force my car back into the left lane. As the Jazz is a small and nimble car, I manged to out accelerate him, with him pulling up at the junction on my left. And the what happened next was that with his skinny build and fugly face, the driver of the bus that had just tried to force me off the road, exits the bus and proceeds walking angrily towards my direction. On seeing this,I reached for my faithful Glock 19 placed in the passenger seat rear pouch with my left hand and held it on my left lap in view of whoever wanted to peer into my car and then lowered my left front window. As the 'hero' neared my left window and lowered his head to swear Thai vulgarities at me and give me his I'm going to 'fuck you up so bad' look, I slowly lifted the Glock up and moved my left hand as if to rest it on the front passenger seat, and on seeing the Glock in my left grip, his faced turned ashen and he hastened his retreat back to his bus and on the lights turning green, sped off. Two things came to mind after the incident. Who was responsible for the said altercation and what would have been the consequences had I lost control of my vehicle and ploughed into some innocent bystanders. As my reactions and judgement of speed are now at an all time low, perhaps I could have been at least partially to blame for the said incident, I concluded that I will not take any unnecessary risks with my driving and to only drive in the event of any emergencies.

16 May – Wtf ???

<u>MAY 16, 2015</u>

It started about 3 hours ago when I was talking to the wife on the phone that I felt a difficulty in speaking, the words just became so difficult to say out and the right side of my throat felt numb. I rushed my speech and ended the call. I tried to get up from the dining chair but felt no feeling in my right leg. So I descended to the floor on my fours and proceeded to drag myself into my bedroom. This had happened once before but tonight it felt more overwhelming, the feeling of paralysis on the right side of my body.

As I pulled myself up into bed, the paralyzing 'sensation' was now accompanied by a strange cramping feeling deep in the muscle. As I lay there I thought for sure that I would not be able to walk or talk again as the muscles in my throat felt like they had 'died' too. I reached for the mobile and Vibered the wife the following, 'very depressed, can't walk and had to crawl to bed'. She calls me almost immediately and asked if I had taken my meds to which I replied in the positive. I then told her that I couldn't talk and we hung up.

So as is usually the case in similar scenarios, depression took over and the urge to do something stupid starts to fester in the mind. As the tears welled up and the paralysis took over the whole right side of my body, I prayed that he would put me out of my misery. Before too long I had fallen asleep and would awake about an hour later feeling almost like before the episode started and began to write this post. It was just so weird, how could one go from feeling like his body had given up on him, to one of normalcy in the space of 3 hours ? Was this going to be the start of a trend ? I have not come across such symptoms of PD before. It just fucks with your mind and consumes all of your being if you let it. It has become a daily war with these little battles I have to go thru with PD, and for sure it's tough, but the support that I have been receiving from family and friends has been amazing, coupled with God's unseen hand, helps me get thru the day...

So perhaps the message that I think God is trying to convey is 'there will be shitty times for sure, but don't do something that will fuck yourself up and always believe that there is always light at the end of the tunnel'.

17 May – Love and other drugs...

MAY 17, 2015

Love is :

- seldom at first sight

- not to be confused with lust

- not being 'in love'

- seeing yourself in your partner's eyes every time you converse

- the blind faith your partner places in you and in every decision that you make

- when she's still there next to you when even that blind faith has been misplaced

- when your voice, opinions, thoughts, secrets, and revelations become the only ones that really mattered

- a mutual sacrifice in personal space, personal thoughts, personal prejudices, personal relationships, and personal well, Self...

- is saying sorry and meaning it. It is not a difficult thing to do and nor will it be implied as accepting defeat

- when after time your interests, hobbies, dreams, wants, diverge but you find your partner still beside you in spite of…

- hard work and a path of thorns and roses

- best embodied in the old, old, old, phrase ' till death do us part "…

Well, my understanding of love anyway…

Lest i forget, love is also that great stick of Dutch weed that makes you fly…

17 MAY 2 – WHAT'S IN A NAME…

MAY 17, 2015

Having to watch your spending especially in the IT and electronics department of any mall is something I have learnt to adapt to since I stopped working about 2 1/2 years ago.

It's a torture to browse the myriad of mobiles, laptops, notebooks and tablets available in the market today and knowing that you have a very prohibitive budget to work with. However, one learns to live within his means and it makes the endeavour more fun [for a masochist] when you have to try to extract every GHz, every Gigabyte, every mega pixel from your purchase with limited funds.

I love Samsung products, but my 2 last purchases, a Samsung A7 mobile and a Samsung Galaxy Tab 3 have been disappointing.

Both seem to be afflicted by an over sensitive touch screen and a laggy user interface especially when scrolling. It does come as a surprise as the processors on both are no sloths and both come with more than adequate RAM and expanded hdd space. Whilst looking for a 7 to 8 inch tab recently, I stumbled across a brand that I had overlooked previously. ASUS is seen as a mainly lower cost PC / tablet maker even though they have a few high end models. I narrowed my search down a 7 incher of moderate tech specs and the 8 inch higher spec'd Memo pad. Both were well within my budget at 4190 baht and 7990 baht respectively. However, after a futile search online for the Memo pad 8 due to it being of stock, I opted for the 7 inch fonepad 7 K0 1N [FE171CG] running dual core Intel Atom Z2520 1.2 GHz and Kit Kat 4.4.2. Off I went to the closest IT shop I know of called IT City in Gateway Ekkamai. No questions asked, I plonked my THB down, grabbed the tab and left the premises almost as quickly as I'd gotten there. On reaching home I unboxed the tab and found a couple of thinly written "manuals" both in Thai, and hence of no use to me. Then came the hardware....looks pretty decent in white and of better finish than my more expensive Samsung Tab 3, I thought to myself. Location of the operational buttons and SIM slots were logical and so I proceeded to boot the mother up...I had earlier inserted 2 SIMs this being a dual SIM gadget.

On simple config of the gadget, it was then time for some fun...On review, I have to say that for a tab cum phone of the sub RM 500 range it is an excellent device with just the right touch sensitivity and hardly any lag in browsing, scrolling or whilst multi tasking. It's not perfect by any means with a display that is less than vibrant and cameras that are both front n back facing but lacking in sharpness and clarity. But with dual facing speakers, the music playback is real good. Wireless connectivity is excellent and text input is not bothersome at all. All 3 of my latest blog postings were on the ASUS and using the WordPress app from play store. My conclusion is that for around RM 450 and on a limited budget you could do much much worse. So it's not difficult for me to say that it's been money well spent...

21 MAY – AWESOME...

<u>MAY 21, 2015</u>

Yesterday was the soft opening for my Bangkok hair salon, Blush, despite feeling extremely tired due to lack of sleep and the PD meds, it turned out to be an awesome first day.

Hopefully I will be able to continue with God at my side and have the energy to sustain the biz.

In the meantime I thank God for his blessings without which this phase of my life would not have been possible.

27 May – Serenity

MAY 26, 2015

It's 2 a.m. here in Bangkok and I've just woken up thinking it's 4 a.m., the time I've been getting up at the past few nights.

It's been a strange sort of week, normally, my head is just constantly processing, or rather trying to anticipate and formulate my next body movement so that I can minimize the number of postural instabilities and falls. The manner in which a normal person gets up from a sitting position at a dinner table, say in a restaurant, to his next destination, for example, towards the cashier's counter to make a payment, is natural and accomplished without any thought or hesitation. A simple enough task that i could have done with my eyes closed, pre-PD. Nowadays it's like, "okay, now don't make a fool of yourself in front of all your fellow diners, and "clear" the table of it's glasses like you've done before, think ! think ! plan your exit so that you may leave the premises with some dignity". No, exaggerate I do not, that is one of the "lifestyle changes" a PD patient must endure. And then, on reaching your destination, i.e. cashier, you open your mouth and "taa_aa__u rai k_k_krap is the best you can muster and the cashier looks a you and wonders " wtf ? is this guy some perv or what ?", it's just a fucked up thing to live with, PD.

However, this week, perhaps due to the excitement of opening my own hair studio, whatever's left of my brain cells that have not been devoured by PD, must be working over time and producing whatever the hell my body needs to move normally, that I seem to be less engrossed in strategizing my next motion and have emerged relatively unscathed, save a few "wobbly" moments, reminders that tell you "don't get over confident and think you're cured you dumb mf, PD will mess you up real bad if you do not take care (of yourself)". I endeavour to stay positive but at the same time not take things for granted, and "I'm gonna make the rest of my life, the best of my life".

So, it's with some hard to fathom, surreal feeling of acquired serenity that I sign off with a verse extracted from almost the end of a video I viewed on 'Whatsapp' – " Love is just a word until somebody comes along and gives it meaning". Incongruous, given the context, but beautiful nevertheless ?

28 May – Just an ordinary day…

MAY 28, 2015

…Got up at 6.30 a.m. and fed Scotty who was meowing like he hadn't eaten in days. Spent the next half hour giving him some TLC that he'd been missing recently. Never thought a cat could be so affectionate, so loving and well, so 'human'. He's got the most beautiful light gold colored eyes and a beautiful coat of fur to match. When I leave for the salon in the morning, he will meow his disapproval and likewise meow with fervor the minute I insert the room key in the door on return, later that night. Love the little fellow.

After a shower, I make my way to Big-C for some groceries and odd and ends for the salon. At around 9.45 a.m. I arrive at the salon where my head stylist (Ms Ptoon) is already there, sweeping up yesterday's hair trimmings which litter the floor. I drop off my knapsack and head for this little stall behind the condo that sells spring rolls (un-fried) with meat and veggies stuffing that come with a rather savory, tangy sauce that has fish sauce as it's main ingredient. Nice ! I ask for 2 packs to go, one for moi and one for Ptoon together with 2 Nescafe ais and all for just 90 baht.

Ptoon was initially un-cooperative and disinterested in her job or rather the new boss, as was somewhat expected. On the 3rd day she says she wants to leave and I said ok and had actually already started to look for a replacement on day 2. However, with the help of Marciano, the previous owner, whom I've become fond of because of his unselfish and selfless personality, we managed to persuade Ptoon to stay for at least a month whilst we searched for a suitable candidate. With the added incentive of a small commission on 3 of the dearer hair treatments that she will receive per customer on top of her basic salary, her attitude and performance has improved markedly and she is doing real good now. I hope she decides to stay longer because she is a 'Jack of all trades' when it comes to hair styling, having worked her way thru hair dressing jobs and owning her own salon until recently.

As owner, I try to avoid touching a customer's locks but a few days ago, Ptoon was late for work (the resent your boss phase) and a young lady walks in for a wash and blow dry. I told the customer that Ptoon will be in soon but after 15 minutes and with Ptoon still missing, I asked the customer if would be ok if I washed her hair. And so began my first experience (no, not THAT kind) of washing a Blush customer's hair. On the second shampooing and on commencement of the conditioning process, in strolls Ptoon and I regretfully hand over the remaining tasks to her. Regretfully because, yes guys, the young lady was quite a cutie

Fast forward to 8 p.m. today and it's been a relatively quiet day and am thankful for the ordinary-ness of today...No PD act ups so far and I hope to get a good night's sleep tonight...

30 May – Ordinary 2

MAY 29, 2015

...6 a.m. Saturday, spent 40 minutes at the gym yesterday morning and managed 5 km on the bike and 2 km on the tread mill. Was expecting and improvement in balance and stability but the result was contrary to my expectations...

I found that with increased fatigue, my balance and ability to initiate forward movement had deteriorated to the extent that I fell forwards later that afternoon and hit the fridge with some force...all through out yesterday and this morning especially when going to the loo, I tread carefully and it's only now, some 24 hours later that I feel much better and am able to walk better, with better balance.

I'm no doctor, but I assume that perhaps my work out yesterday morning was a little too intense, and I shall hit the gym again after this post but with a more sedate work out and see what happens.

It was a good day at the salon yesterday, almost matching our highest daily takings of a week ago, hope it continues and the ladies keep a coming to our hair studio. So far the nails section has seen no action and I hope to complete our flyer soon to try and advertise our services more, that way. Thanks guys for listening...

2 JUNE – SORRY TO BURST YOUR BUBBLE, BUT YOU'RE FUCKED…

JUNE 2, 2015

…Short post as my mind is just in a whirl and I am just so thoroughly fed up with this fucking disease…

A good few days at the gym and these 'ordinary' few days were so good that that I'd felt as though my PD was in the past. And then out of the blue as I was exiting the bathroom at about 9.15 p.m. tonight, my left leg or both legs (can't remember now) froze and I fell forwards leaning left and hit the ground hard. Almost a carbon copy of my fall in Seoul, except this time I broke the fall with my left hand and fractured my wrist. Didn't see that coming and whilst the pain is bearable, thoughts flow thru my mind like 'what would have happened if I had hit my head on something ?'

So my mind is currently aching more than my wrist and sorry fellow PD sufferers but cycling, I surmise, does shit all for PD…

2 June 2 – To give a fuck ?...

JUNE 2, 2015

Couldn't sleep as the pain while bearable was well, still a pain...

On hindsight, after crashing into my fridge on 30 May, perhaps I could have been more careful ? I am already as things are now, constantly thinking about my movement and forward motion and it's really exhausting, so how do I make my brain stay alert 24/7 ?

Well I won't because my life would become a meaningless existence in fear ! So God, you know that whilst my belief is still strong, I'd rather not bother going thru whatever's left of my life this way. It's getting tougher for me to believe that there is a reason for all this shit . So please I pray reveal it to me soon... it's ever so easy to accept defeat and to just go away...

9 JUNE – GOD ?

<u>JUNE 9, 2015</u>

…Thank you for the years already given and for the remaining ones left. I don't say it enough but thanks God for making me the person I am. And thank you Mr Tom Chan for being my God's messenger…

10 JUNE – AS IF THERE WAS SOMETHING BETTER TO DO...

<u>JUNE 10, 2015</u>

Underrated

Love – The greatest gift one person (read person) could ever give to another

Children – The second (?) greatest gift the woman you love could ever give to you

Sex – Single most pleasurable physical experience a person could have

Parents – Always taken for granted, frequently ignored, seldom appreciated, UNTIL they are no longer around

Purpose – Without which, we'd all be ships without rudders

Loving your vocation – After spending hours commuting to and from work, the least we would expect of our own choices (of jobs)

Psychological well being – When you frequently drift in and out of depression, it's time to come to your senses (there will be times when you are coherent) and seek some help divinely or humanly, otherwise life will seem, well, unlivable.

Money – as much as we hate to admit it, money is one of the most important things in life, without which life would be pretty shitty and thoroughly boring.

Death – When you are at the end of your journey, your body failing to listen to your mind and your mind, well, has a mind of it's own, you will be glad that your god will recognize your time's up and do something about it.

Well that's my UR list for now, overrated to come…

18 JUNE – OF RUDE PILFERING LADIES, RANTS AND THEN SOME PERSPECTIVE…

JUNE 18, 2015

…Been a while since I've posted and it's that it's been a real tough week for me PD wise, where i'm constantly now struggling with getting up from a sitting or laying down position. And on successfully standing up, the next shit that hits me is that I'd then fall forward. It's like 'fuck me !', my threshold for putting up with this shit is damn near reached. You know, someone sent me this message"

God didn't promise days without pain, laughter without sorrow, or sun without rain, but He did promise strength for the day, comfort for the tears, and light for the way. If God brings you to it, He will bring you through it.

and I went like ""what the fuck !", FUCKING great !

Really, the sender's intentions were noble and I thank you and apologize profusely in advance, but if there was any more of this shit I'd have to digest at this moment in time, I would rather get fucked and die.

I feel like I'm some decrepit and REALLY, I kid you not, it feels like shite. And it's been this black hole that I've been stuck in till today. And then I call up an ex-colleague of mine to ask her for a favor and she tells me that she is on long medical leave as she has just been diagnosed with breast cancer. Somewhere in the middle of the conversation she asks how I am, and I replied, "I'm ok, but not so good with the PD but how are YOU ? The thoughts about me struggling with my PD now on some back burner in my brain. The conversation continued and I felt that at the other end of the line was a strong woman who must be fighting so much pain and uncertainty and that I could take a leaf out of her book. So to Dear Ms KXX, if you are reading this, please stay strong and you shall prevail…

So some perspective thrown in, some semblance of sanity restored, I end this post with a quote which I feel is apt for those of us in our 50s (and beyond)

"I no longer live in time, I live in moments"

…to be continued…with the lady tale…

23 June – Of rude, pilfering ladies....

...I thought I had managed to rehabilitate my previous head stylist, but unfortunately she preferred to remain as the classless, rude, unrefined and pilfering lady that she was.

I had tried my best to make her feel needed and valued as an employee but she wanted to continue to exhibit her "you can't run your hair styling biz without me" attitude, among her other intolerable traits and so I decided to get rid of this cancer that was holding me to perceived ransom. My new head stylist is a Malaysian who speaks fluent Thai and over the short time that Casey's been with Blush he's earned the praises of customers for his styling skills and pleasant demeanor. I hope Casey stays for longer than the 4 months he's promised me as I believe he is an asset to Blush.

I have also added a new stylist to the team and she starts this morning and I hope she too will contribute to the growth of Blush. For sure it's not easy running your own biz, but it can be quite gratifying in some masochistic way.

I end my post today by saying that my liberal use of politically incorrect adjectives, nouns, terminologies and the 'F' word is just me being me and I would not change me. But I can understand if a reader takes offence to the language used, so if you are one of said readers, feel free to ignore my future posts.

Cheers !!

26 June – GOD ? Hmm...

"Is God willing to prevent evil, but not able? Then he is not omnipotent.
Is he able, but not willing? Then he is malevolent.
Is he both able and willing? Then whence cometh evil?
Is he neither able nor willing? Then why call him God?"

– EPICURUS

... The word God is for me nothing more than the expression and product of human weaknesses, the Bible a collection of honourable, but still primitive legends which are nevertheless pretty childish. No interpretation no matter how subtle can (for me) change this. These subtilised interpretations are highly manifold according to their nature and have almost nothing to do with the original text.

– ALBERT EINSTEIN

Well, there had to come a time...

26 June 2 – GOD ? Hmm..2

JUNE 26, 2015

…Your beliefs are your beliefs and i do not possess the inclination to change your point of view on religion, god or life in general and whatever has been expressed on my blog are what I feel are my most personal thoughts, beliefs and just sometimes expressions of frustrations. I do not for the slightest, also want to come across as patronising nor I do not seek sympathy nor charity. If I have inadvertently caused any discomfort, I apologize but recognize that one also has alternative options…

Documenting how I live my life with PD has, I feel, been a sometimes painful and emotionally draining, but mostly revitalising experience up till recently. I also hope that by sharing, fellow PD sufferers might perhaps feel that they are not alone in their fight.

A buddy who knows me well once commented that my blog postings were "brutally' honest. Honest to god, my posts are acutely self-restrained already and to be a 100% honest would be caustically and depressingly honest and unnecessary. So, with all my "disclaimers" out of the way, please read on…

There was an age when if you were fortunate (or unfortunate) enough to be brought up by two loving individuals, your perception of life would be somewhat closeted or shielded from the unpleasant realities. Then you come of age and gradually over years and decades you become enlightened, streetwise, weary, jaded and spent. If you had a god, or rather an unwavering, strong religious belief, the journey perhaps would not take such a route but then again what exactly is god ? To me, simplistically, he (yes, he) was always the person I could turn to in times of need, the "voice" of reason or conscience, and always the resolver. On elemental reflection, my life has been, on the surface, absent of emotional dramas and that is perhaps attributable to my belief that some supreme being is looking after (over) me and guiding me. On closer scrutiny, my life has not been plain sailing with many self-imposed memory lapses and blog non-disclosures. But the biggie that no amount of self-imposing or self-belief or mind over matter training can remove from my daily existence for the last 4 years has been PD. This all-consuming progressive (yes, the fucking progress sometimes scares the shit out of me) degenerative brain disease, has drained me physically especially over these last 3 months where a more apt description of my physical condition would be decrepit. In-spite-of, my belief had still been strong, even to the extent that all this was for a reason which would be revealed in time, as always.

But you know, you get tired, so so so tired, physically and ultimately mentally, and you ask " god, when will the reason be known, when will I know, when will all this pain end, if you really love your son, why must you put him through this shit. Are YOU even there ?" And I have perhaps reached my threshold for physical and emotional pain. Suicide ? been there, done that (with obvious last minute medical intervention), not fun believe you me. So next step, blame god for all that's wrong with my life. So doubts creep in, slowly but surely until... well you just give up on believing, and fuck me, perhaps a more solitary, and quicker attempt is the answer after all...

11 July – Blame Who ???

JULY 10, 2015

…A wise "young" uncle once told me, 'Never explain your actions, live your life one day at a time'.

What exactly did he mean ? In the context of our conversation, I believe what he was trying to tell me was, 'Never try to justify your actions / re-actions by apportioning blame for every repugnant incident in your life. Just take the blows and get on with your life'.

It is ever so easy to blame others (including God) for the perceived misfortunes that befall us, that way we still feel better with ourselves and thus remain 'perfect' and untainted.

Of course there are times when there really is someone else who is actually to be blamed and for those times I suppose a few cursory 'F' words directed at said 'blaimant' would be ok.

So I hope to execute what has been advised to me and be the 'bigger man', easier said than done but I shall give it a shot…

With 4 falls in 2 weeks and injuring my previously fractured wrist again, it pushed me so close to ending it all. Your mind just gets caught up in all the negativity and self-pity and you feel like its easier to just go away then to continue with such an existence.

The phobia of falling had dug itself deep into my psyche and the physical pain experienced from the falls had been bad and on the eve of my flight back to BKK, I decided to pay my KL neuro, Dr Lee Moon Keen a visit. Ever the calming figure and ever the optimist, Dr Lee tells me in no uncertain terms that to even consider suicide was a STUPID thing to do and it is now easier to treat PD. With that said, she proceeds to prescribe a drug called STALEVO which contains L-dopa. I was advised to extend my stay in KL for a week so that she could monitor and fine tune the dosage but I had to leave for BKK as the salon was missed by me. On writing this post, I had taken my first dose of my new meds and so far so good. Will update the mid to long-term effectiveness of this new drug at a later time...

19 July – 5 Gen of Male Taits (from GTJ perspective)

JULY 19, 2015

John James Tait

George Tait

Sonny Tait

George Tait Jr

Aeyden James Tait

19 July 2 – An experiment almost gone awry...

JULY 19, 2015

...Yesterday morning was the last dose of the new drug I'm taking before going on to one of a higher dosage.

Logically, I was to continue my second and third new higher dosages at Lunch and Dinner yesterday. Being the wise ass that I am, I decided to skip both dosages and opted to start my higher dosages at Breakfast this morning... Fuuuuck !!! I suspected something was not right when I got up for one of my many "P" expeditions at about 4 a.m. and my legs felt weak. Thinking that perhaps it was just tiredness, I went back to sleep with similar results from the subsequent expeditions. It was at 10.30 a.m. when I finally got up but COULDN'T !!! It was like I was paralysed with both feet buckling under me and my arms were so bloody weak and accompanied by just general intense fatigue. Scared the shit out of me and I proceed to crawl toward my new Tabs on the computer table in the hall and quickly downed my new dose with just my saliva (desperate times call for desperate measures) and prayed (yes..) for the best. Within 15 minutes the sensation of power returned to my limbs and the rest of my body and within a hour I was back cleaning up my condo...

So fellow PD sufferers don't mess with your dosages...

30 JULY – DO YOU BELIEVE IN GOD? – THE POWER OF PRAYER AND THE POWER OF CHRIST...

JULY 30, 2015

The past few months have seen me degenerate physically, into a decrepit and emotionally into a lost spirit.

My belief in God had all but expired and it became simply a black or white decision on whether I wanted to continue to exist or to just extinguish what was left of GTJ.

And then a little voice told me to come home to see my neuro for a last stab at a flicker of hope...and with that came the usual trial and error exercise in finding the perfect dosage that I could cope with and the usual up and downs and bouts of depression...BUT you know, perhaps you have to hit rock bottom in order to realize that we are not the products of "The Big Bang Theory" nor are we the result or the consequence of any "Theory of Evolution". The scientists among you who are reading this would probably be thinking "ignorant simpleton" but believe me that I had an "A" in my favorite science subject Physics so...

I believe I was at my lowest ebb in my life last night when I did the unthinkable. Please note that I have not gone fucking crazy as I tell you what I did ; I prayed to Jesus Christ and acknowledged or perhaps it was more like apologized vehemently to him for my public doubting of his existence and then calmly and with a trace of resignation that belied the positive emotion and faith that

66

whatever I was about to ask of him, he would deliver…, I promised that if he did indeed grant me a second chance, I would use it to help other Parkinson's patients by speaking on the trials and tribulations that come with PD and how to cope with it (from my honest perspective) and volunteer my services to anyone or any society or health organization that would have me.

And so, it was a DIVINE REVELATION to me (I wish I could be more specific but just please take my word for it) today that he had answered my prayer and if I ever doubted his existence, this was surefire proof that God DOES exist and he DOES listen…

With this I hope that my blog ends its run here in its current form and constitution and perhaps sometime in the future, something more spiritually uplifting will metamorphosize from it…

10 AUG – A NEW BEGINNING ?

<u>AUGUST 9, 2015</u>

I hesitate to say this but I think I'm done with my PD Blog therapy…I hope I have managed to reach out to fellow sufferers and their caregivers and alleviated any pain or uncertainty with whatever little I had to offer in terms of my postings…

I have no idea what I'm going to be blogging about now but somehow I still feel good, optimistic, refreshed and above all spiritually rejuvenated enough to continue posting on whatever comes to mind.

For a start, I thought I'd take a stab at creating or writing meaningful quotes; those short, concise expressions of whatever occurrences or thoughts that crossed my mind during the day that was worth penning down. I hope it connects with some and sometimes if these quotes do seem like they are directed at any person real or imagined, well, it just is…please take my last statement with a barrel of salt ya ?

Thanks for listening n I attach my first 2 quotes for your enjoyment (?)…

"Underneath one's facade dwells another realm and domain that even one's beloved soul mate could never begin to fathom; therein lies a man's deepest and most lurid rationalizations"

gtj

"He who believes the dross he dishes out is the be-all and end-all of life is the self-righteous preacher of probity whose only claim to fame and affirmation would be, his hypocrisy"

gtj

15 August – LOVE is.....

"Love is, the unadulterated emotion that unleashes passion, the pain that tramples your spirit, the ambiguity that sweeps the mind, the source of piety and he root of infidelity. Love, it takes you to blissful ethereal places and down murky depths you never knew" LOVE is.......
gtj

LOVE is many things to many people.....

16 August – Home...

AUGUST 16, 2015

"Home beckons, some days, though the lure gets weaker by the day,

Home, Oh dear home, where art thou?,

Home....it is in the mind, where turmoil antecedently resided, where resolutions and finality realize,

Home is where my heart is...."

gtj

16 August – The raging tempests in my mind…

"Dissect if you must, probe till perpetuity,

Chaos, conflicts and contradictions take wing thru my mind

like a violent tempest,

And it's bleak outside, too bleak to fly,

So persist if you must, pursue if you dare,

Nihility will unfold,

And it's bleak outside, too bleak to fly, too bleak to die…" gtj

3/9 – SO, WHAT NOW, MR TAIT ?

SEPTEMBER 3, 2015

Yes, I know the blog is supposed to be dead and buried but some things just can't be expressed concisely, quote wise...so please indulge me...

So what am I going to lady about, I thought...surely something must be bothering me enough to want to go through the roller coaster ride again.

An awful fucking lot actually, but some things too caustic to be said about too many persons (myself included, yes it's been that kind of 'fuck me' day) that it would have degenerated into an exercise in recrimination...

So just calm down, think aloud, think slowly and stay focused, I keep telling myself...so the trick would be to say much without truly saying anything, I thought... easy peasy !

No, but really I've just been going thru my posts since day 1 and it's been somewhat 'useful' to me to know that I've documented what I've been thru since April 2015 and helps me relive some nice times and some fucked up ones too. But wtf, that's life isn't it, no one said it would be a bed of roses...anyways so I'm feeling awkwardly strange today like my mind is there but not quite there if you know what I mean...and its a muddle of thoughts, maybe I'm just super duper tired ... and oh, btw, I just had 2 tats done yesterday... please see accompanying pics...and so before the original intention of my re-blogging, i sign off and wish everyone a pleasant day...

9/9 – MY DEAR AUNTS...PART 1

SEPTEMBER 9, 2015

There are people I'm sure who have one time or another touched another's life and it is not often that one takes the time and effort to perhaps say a little thank you to these special people...

My dad being a Police Officer was constantly on the move, being transferred from one state to another was quite the norm, and my mum would also follow dad to wherever he was posted. I was born in Penang and attended up to Primary school year 1 there, and I remember during the times when my parents were moving from one place to another, there were periods of time that I did not tag along and was left to the care of my aunty Rosalind.

Dear aunty Rosalind is a quiet, caring lady who loved me like her own son, like the son she never had. Her story is a sad and quite tragic one as she had lost the one man she truly loved at a young age and never really recovered from that experience. So as not to dredge up old wounds, the circumstances surrounding her heartbreaking experience shall remain suppressed. But it was a romance like from days gone by...the man she loved was my father's brother John, also in the Police force, also a handsome dashing young man like dad used to be. When he died she carried the sadness with her eternally, sometimes nightmares of his death would overcome her and I remember those times vividly as I slept next to her nights, for nearly 7 years of my life. She would choose to remain unmarried and it goes without saying how much I respect her for the woman she is, for the immense love that she had for uncle John, for her undying devotion and dedication to his memory...and for the selfless and uncomplaining character that she possessed and for devoting 7 years of her life to caring for and loving her sister's son…

My early childhood memories naturally revolve around her, like how she used to wake me up many many times during the night to go to the loo, thus disrupting her own sleep in the process and how she used to change my trouser jammies in the middle of the night on those occasions that she was a wee bit late in leading me to the loo…how she used bark at anyone who had uttered a bad thing to or about me…how her eyes lit up and she would smile whenever she was talking to me…how she'd give me anything I asked for without question…how her laugh would always perk me up and how her eyes would well up with tears whenever it was time for me to go away on a long trip with my parents…

My dearest dearest aunty Rosalind aka mama…, please forgive me if I have forgotten about you or of your contributions to the fondest memories of my childhood…please forgive me for forgetting what a special person you are and have been and please forgive God for the Alzeimer's that he has I'm sure unintentionally given you…I would finally like to say "thank you" for being there during that period in my life…

28/9 – A VERY BLUNT ASSESSMENT CUM CONFESSION…

<u>SEPTEMBER 28, 2015</u>

It should have been a good week for me after arriving back in KL on the 25 Sep 2015, for my son Aeyden's graduation.

It was yesterday that he received his scroll at his graduation ceremony and I shall always be thankful to God that both my kids now have the opportunity to start their working lives at a comfortable level.

Just as Aeyden's life now truly begins, and so, mine is perhaps heading in the opposite direction…

To the non-PD sufferer or skeptic, what I am about to say next may seem like "oh yes, blame your flaws on PD again". And to a certain extent that is true. The vices are the same, but the reasons for them are multi-faceted.

There comes a time when you tire of popping pills and observing dosage timings that you couldn't give a shit anymore. So the falls return, the pain both physical and mental, return, the need to dull or suppress or to forget the fucking pain returns too. And then it starts by " how about I go to Mojos for a couple of hours and get a little high from both the alcohol and the ever present female company ?" Then stagger home at some ungodly hour with all thoughts and pain related to whatever the fuck ailment you tell yourself you are suffering from, all but a distant memory.

And it would be still acceptable too (to me at least) if it was intelligently perceived by one as a one-off remedy. However, in my case it has gone on for too often and for too long. And when it carries over to your holidays back home too, then things will ultimately come to a head. And so it has…when your partner of 32 years runs out of patience and can only tolerate so much of your perceived PD symptoms (or more likely, excuses) for your behavior, when your apologies and false promises no longer mean a fucking thing…

Before anyone jumps to any conclusions about my current state of mind and hence state of MIS-behavior, I would categorically state here and now that Pre-PD, I was never the person I am now. Well only God truly knows…

So what exactly the point of this post ? Well, if I could live my life for another person at this moment in my life, I would. But I can't, not when I'm in constant mental and often physical pain and whatever remains of my life could very easily be taken away just by a fall and a blow to my fucking skull…and so the point is, if any of you is ever facing a similar to mine, please do try to do it better than I have and not to hurt anyone that you value like I have…

3/10 – OF POLITICS AND POLITICIANS...

OCTOBER 3, 2015

NIRVANA

Formal politics is politics as defined by law. Essentially, everyone follows the rules. One man, one vote, everyone follows the rule of law, people can petition their government for wrongs and have them heard, and so on. It involves the collective action of individuals in pursuit of common goals Formal politics involves individual or collective action in public forums, social movements, media, citizens' groups, or political parties.

REALITY BITES

Informal politics, in developing countries, tends to undermine the rule of law by creating a tendency towards corruption and cronyism. Paying a bribe to get a hearing is an example of informal politics. So is talking to your tribal elder (through family channels) when he also happens to be a judge or senior government official.

SUPER NIRVANA

A **politician** (from <u>Classical Greek</u> πόλις, "<u>polis</u>") is a person holding or seeking an office within a <u>government</u>, usually by means of an election, voted for either by people or by a definitive group in the government. A person experienced in the art or science of government; *especially* : one actively engaged in conducting the business of a government. [1]Politicians propose, support and create laws or policies that govern the land and, by extension, its people.

Broadly speaking, a "politician" can be anyone who seeks to achieve <u>political</u> <u>power</u> in any <u>bureaucratic</u> institution where the ranks are awarded by the kind of support the person has.

REALITY BITES OUR ARSE

A person actively engaged in politics, esp. party politics, professionally or otherwise; often, a person holding or seeking political office: ***frequently used in a derogatory sense, with implications of seeking personal or partisan gain***, scheming, opportunism, etc.

SUPER DUPER NIRVANA ?

Anarchy – absence of government and absolute freedom of the individual, regarded as a political ideal.

26/10 -FINISHED !! OF "FRIENDS", HYPOCRISY, COURAGE, THE "SALESMAN", THE TRUE FRIEND...PART 1

OCTOBER 25, 2015

The Oxford dictionary defines a Friend as :

1. A person with whom one has a bond of mutual affection, typically one exclusive of sexual or family relations: eg. *'she's a friend of mine'*, *'we were close friends'*
2. Used as a polite form of address or in ironic reference) an acquaintance or a stranger one comes across: eg. *my friends, let me introduce myself*
3. A person who supports a cause, organization, or country by giving financial or other help: eg. *the Friends of the Welsh National Opera*

The Free Dictionary defines a Friend as :

4. A person whom one knows, likes, and trusts.

The Casual Friend

A "Friend" then to me would be – 1) of the Oxford dict. definition, a very simplistic relationship, where there only exists a bond of mutual affection.

The categories would be FB, old school mates, office colleagues and other acquaintances.

The TRUE Friend

However True FRIENDS to me would be :

– a non-judgmental friend who will support you no matter what. This is the kind of friend who knows you are in a hot mess and knows all of your deepest and darkest secrets, but still loves you all the same.

However, he / she should also be intelligent enough to review his support for you in situations where it involves for example, a dispute between yourself and your spouse. He should be able to distinguish between who is right and who is wrong and be direct and courageous enough to castigate you if it was blatantly obvious you were in the wrong.

Conversely, there are certain situations in life where we need to hear the harsh truth. That's what the brutally honest confidant is for. If you're in a rocky relationship and everyone's telling you that it's perfectly normal that you're back with that special someone for the 8th time in the last 2 years, the brutally honest confidant is there to yank your rose-colored glasses off and tell you, "Enough. Stop with all that break-up-and-get-back-together drama. You deserve better." Friends are supposed to be honest with each other.

The Hypocrite "FRIEND"

And then there's the friend of the spouse who is also supposedly your friend as well :

One who on the exterior asks about your health and your well being like she really cares but internally plots your breakup with your spouse.

This kind of friend is most **despicable** kind whose blind support for your spouse can almost cause the break up of your marriage. Granted, the feed back for the spouse might be an influential factor but come on, surely with armed with a degree from England, one can't be so fucking stupid, can one ? And not to mention the hypocrisy in pretending to be concerned about the health of the spouse's partner.

Similarly, **beware** YOUR "Friend" who views the condition of your spousal relationship as your fault and instead of having the "balls" to at least approach you for answers, goes ahead and supports your spouse instead. Friends like these are dismissed and not missed at all.

26/10 – FINISHED !! – FRIENDS PART 2

OCTOBER 25, 2015

The "Salesman" Friend

What can I say about this category ? The kind who opens his mouth and says everything will be alright and if you need help go to him and all will be ok.

Well, when you actually approach said friend for help, excuses are the only things forthcoming !! *Laughable* if not for the history of your relationship with this friend going back decades.

And there is the perennial liar who has his redeeming qualities where, when he is not feeding you garbage and lies, is really a decent human being who goes out of his way to help with tasks and assists wherever and whenever he can with any of your requests except the fucker just can't stop lying. Go figure ! But I am still able love this perennial liar.

So, over these 54 years of existence I've come across all sorts of characters .I am by no means perfect but at least I have the "balls" to air my views and open myself up to constructive critique.

26/10 – FINAL – FRIENDS PART 3

OCTOBER 25, 2015

With reference to my article FRIENDS Part 1, specifically the hypocrite Friend,

I wish said person the full impact of Newton's Third Law :

"For every action, there is an equal and opposite reaction ."

Yeah, rot in hell LADY !!!

We come into this world alone and we leave it, alone...

A great article by Paul Hudson :

At The End Of The Day You Are Alone

Life should NOT be a journey to the grave with the intention of arriving safely in an attractive and well preserved body, but rather to skid in sideways, body thoroughly used up, totally worn out, screaming, "WOOHOO What A Ride!"

29/10 – MORTALITY AND OTHER INCONSEQUENTIAL MUSINGS....

OCTOBER 29, 2015

The realization of one's mortality and the transient nature of our existence does wonders to one's psyche.

If we are blessed by the almighty to have attained a decent age and led a "meaningful" life, by the grace of his compassion and understanding of the person you were, are or will become, then it would have all been worth it, the journeys of physical and mental hurt, the neuropsychiatric bouts as a consequence of a progressive degenerative disorder, the pain of dealing with the loss of a parent and an assuaging voice, the joys and joys (yes, not a typo) of bringing up 2 kids, the uncertainties of embarking on a solo excursion, the futile resistance to the finality of death.

Morbid as it sounds, it does induce one to try to live one's remaining years on one's terms and to go out in a blaze of glory....

4/11 – Do I give a shit anymore ? No, not really...

<u>NOVEMBER 3, 2015</u>

To be continued...

4/11 – SORRY FOR ANY CONFUSION RELATED TO THE TITLE OF MY PREVIOUS POST "DO I GIVE A SHIT? NO, NOT REALLY…"

NOVEMBER 4, 2015

Its actually to be the title of a forthcoming post and unrelated to any of my previous posts. Apologies…

3/1/2016 – A FALL A DAY....

Thank you my dear cousins, aunties, sister, and friends for all your words of support, encouragement throughout the years for Mr Crazy.

From my recent FB posts I think the general perception is that PD has taken such a toll on me physically (and hence psychologically) that I would feel better dead. That is true, and although Ii'd like to leave that decision solely to GOD, I can't honestly say that I will...

What follows will be as true an account of my journey thru life since being diagnosed with Parkinson's Disease as I dare document.

It is not an exercise in justifications, blame, excuses, the soliciting of pity nor narcissism. It will be as real an account of the physical and mental pain that I go thru on a daily (yes, daily) basis especially over this last year and how I manage them.

Resurrection of this blog is also to put things straight and not for the purpose of the "airing dirty laundry".

Firstly, I'd state my wife of 29 years is not even remotely responsible for this path that my life has taken, nor is GOD.

She was perhaps the one true force that could have saved me, if she'd known how...but how could she when i myself did not know or want to know... I hope she is able to forgive me for all I've been (or not been) to her for the last 35 years that we've known each other.

GOD, My God, Dearest Jesus, who has been with me for as long as I remember. The one entity in my life that I thought was creating this path for me that would ultimately lead to his final and most awesome gift / revelation to me, one of lasting happiness, contentment, one where whatever was missing or what i thought was missing from my life was finally attained. He has without a doubt saved my ass so many times, more times than I deserve, and my faith though at times wavered, never ceased. And so, perhaps only on my death bed will I know what his true intentions for me were.

And then there was me…me, this organism that was created, but for what ? An accidental freak of nature, an insignificant byproduct of Genesis or just a flawed man who through his limited range of emotions and psychological attributes tries to justify the merits of his existence and perhaps try to help others who are in a similar environment by sharing ?

Well, FXXX me if I know…but what I do know is that I have a conscience, even though not always obvious and that accompanied by the fear of being labelled a hypocrite and also the hope that by sharing, it will maybe help me reconcile my life, maybe the only reasons for this post…

to be continued…

9/1/2016 – A COUPLE OF JOINTS WOULD BE GREAT RIGHT NOW...

<u>JANUARY 9, 2016</u>

The mind is foggy N boggy today, so trudging through all the crap is going to be an effort for sure. So let's start the lazy man's way, by cheating a little, i.e. by summary, bullets or no elaboration at all...

Feeling extremely tired N totally lacking in mental composure, alertness N any feeling of compassion (for myself or anyone else) I submit myself to this exercise in masochism...

In a time & space not so long ago, *I COULD* :

1. WALK or just stand up without falling over on a daily basis
2. After pausing to sit or lie down then get back on my feet with no effort at all.
3. TALK without the stammer, lisps, low volume and with the speed of ...(Carl Lewis)
4. Eat using a fork N knife or a fork N spoon
5. Write
6. Sign my signature (which will lead me to the story of my encounter with a lady Thai immigration officer the last time I came back to BKK)
7. Hold my temper (debatable, I know)
8. FXXX like a Duracell bunny .
9. Go through the day, without feeling like my eyes would just suddenly shut N my brain, would shut down on me.

10. Get up just one morning, just one morning feeling good, energized, pain free both physically N mentally.

1, 2, 3, 9 & 10 being the worst or the biggest loss in physical ability that affects me. And if anyone tells you, to stay strong, fight the fight, don't give up....*it's truly, truly appreciated* but I know as sure as there is a hell, I will not want to struggle on, not worth the ever gnawing pain, and that is the honest truth…

I have come terms with my life, the trials and tribulations, the good and the fucking worst, the feelings of alone-ness (no not in Oxford's), the feelings of abundance N blessedness and when it's time to shut the lights off, I will be ready…no regrets and as Frankie said "I did it……….."

And of GOD, thanks for you guys for your spiritual support but just 2 points to ponder :

Someone(s) quoted me the following which I attach an extract :

1.   "GOD is with you and HE is in control.."
−   sorry to politely debunk this and the justification for my opinion is for another day..
2.   2. "PD does not define you"
−   sorry but it does, to the Nth degree and the justification….etc etc

to be continued…..

19/1 – THE DAY ACCOUNTABILITY CAME A KNOCKING...

I have never really regretted anything I've done as I've always viewed my actions from my perception (& perspective).

As long as I was satisfied with the subsequent results of my actions (and damn the consequences to anyone else) I'd dwell no further on it and move on....

So, today is the day I come clean to GOD and (to my loved ones & anyone else who felt I've wronged them in the past) and be accountable for possessing what I believe are the greatest relationship killers and character downfalls to a man or woman, SELFISHNESS & DENIAL.

Why now ? Because after a brief but meaningful whatsapp conversation with a believer who has always posted very positive religious quotes on my FB pages, it became very clear that here was not my nnnnnn-in-law at the other end of the line but the said person's mode and line of questioning and replies were of a GREATER design, well, only she will know if it was a divine moment

And the topic of conversation was my impending Divorce...

to be continued

20/1 – ACCOUNTABILITY HAS LEFT THE BUILDING...

<u>JANUARY 20, 2016</u>

Simply, the continuation of my current post ceases as the intention of my said post has been (mis)interpreted to be some grand plan conceived by an evil mind to twist and distort facts to my benefit. (Just saying....)

21/1 – The Caregiver…truly special human being and as rare as a white lion (not seen since 1994)…well, some of us have not seen a CG since…

<u>JANUARY 21, 2016</u>

Please GOD give me the courage to exit before i get to his stage (Pls see<u>E8https://youtu.be/AtRF9koKVE8</u>

2/2 -DIVORCE, WELL, WHAT CAN I SAY....

FEBRUARY 1, 2016

Its strange when a relationship comes to an end, how the bystanders pick a side, like as if it's something they have to do to "display" their "love" and "loyalty" to their friend or relative.

And naturally the guy i.e. myself will be the obvious scoundrel in the Pantomime, the guy who was this controlling freak, who loses his temper easily, whose erratic behavior bordered on the fringes of the psychotic, the guy whose only focus in life after his 2 kids came into existence, was to try to provide the best he could for them in terms of their childhood and their tertiary education, the guy who might have lost his "Relationship" compass a a little whilst struggling with ensuring that his family got the comforts in life they deserved, all the while mindful of the finances that would be required in the retirement years.

So the scoundrel would be further admonished when he, on being diagnosed with a serious progressive degenerative disease in later years, decided that he had fulfilled his responsibilities as a parent with 2 graduate children and went on a hiatus to find his lost self....Selfish bastard ! Irresponsible parent ! Philandering husband !...

On return from his hiatus, he had in his head worked out a comprehensive retirement plan that would have supported both spouses in later years (dependent on both parties' willingness to tighten their belts and sacrifice).

Needless to say said plan did not stand a chance for implementation as ....well that's almost as far as i would go to "airing dirty laundry" and will let the "bystanders" in on a few hints :

a)   Instigator and Hypocrite
b)   schemers
c)   e-mail correspondences
d)   temporary respite
e)   back up plan or disaster recovery plan was what we used to call it in Alliance bank
f)   Acceptance of accountability – To be sure, subsequently, the scoundrel went on this spree of unmentionable and unforgivable deeds that would....well, as John sung....IMAGINE...

Well that fucking camel had to be off my back...

Thank you for reading....there is no right or wrong in this drama, just....xxx

3/2 – Moving on…

It's been a pretty eventful fortnight and here's to many more (and so I say with a Chang in hand – Mr A.M. I'm missing you…).

Well, let's quickly move on from the PAST & not look back for time being.

It's been quite an exciting few days browsing the various web sites like EBay and Lazada Thailand, looking for "stuff" to enhance my inventory as well as put some money into a second "distraction" which I hope will turn out to be sustainable (as in interest & derived pleasures) hobby that will keep my mind from just focusing on one issue the whole day i.e. the thought of PD and its accompanying shite.

Hobby numero uno : Digital Photography.

I have had an interest in analogue photography since my childhood days, however due to costs and focusing on trying to attain a higher education (yes and look where that got me eh ?) the interest had waned and throughout adult life, the usual expenses like household and….and….and….. the budget was never quite there to prod me into jumping into it.

Thankfully at the Grand old age of xxx, and with my retirement budget pretty much sorted out and taking into account little surprise budget bumps along the way (watch this space…) it seems like a good time to get my mind straight and focus on pleasures (of non-carnal nature), that would help in the banishment and progressive elimination of negative thoughts from my head.

Digital photography has come a long way since it came into existence god knows how long ago and the technology behind it has jumped to levels beyond my abilities to comprehend the concept 100 %, but hey, i try and try and it feels sometimes like i'm going back to school…just memorizing the tech terminologies alone can make me cringe with apprehension somewhat like one was preparing to sit for an exam ….(yeah, WTF right ?) But it helps to remain calm and tell myself this could be fun and rewarding from a personal achievement pov (yes, way too much porn). And so i invest a couple of K's in the project and hope to well, if anything, to be on my way to healing my mind and soul…

I hope not bore you guys with to much of what may, on the surface, appear as self indulgence but open your minds and join me into the….twilight zone… Nah !! Joke-lah.

Anyways, will continue with my ramblings another time, and i have posted a few pics of what i have tried to capture and pls be kind when viewing the pics as it is a Novice's first attempt at creative photography. The pics also give an idea of what my second hobby is,,,,

Cheers !!! everyone.. (yes one beer too many)

5/2 – Bye to this site of shite and welcome to www.georgetaitjr.com !

Dear all,

Thanks for following my posts on PD, but it's time for a major change in MINDSET and hopefully i will rid myself of all this old PD shite.

So here's to www.georgetaitjr.com !

cheers everyone !!! Go on, get pissed !!

"One's dignity
may be
assaulted,
vandalized
and cruelly
mocked, but
it can never
be taken away
unless it is
surrendered."

Michael J. Fox

30/10 – A RESURRECTION OF SORTS

So it's been 8 months since my last post, and a lot has occurred during that period, the most significant, being the birth of my second daughter (and third child), Natascha Shan-ya Tait.

I know i had mentioned during the cessation of my "old" wordpress blog that, from the inception of my new domain only positives would prevail in my life and hence my posts, TILL NOW....

But as we all know, if only life were that simple, if only life were a bed of roses, if only life elapsed the way we intended it to....so, I intend to, as in my previous guise of **www.georgetaitjr.wordpress.com**, document as honestly as I care to, the happenings in my life (happy or otherwise), my thoughts and opinions on any shite that I feel I need to opine or express, and my daily "war" with PD, EXPLETIVES not withstanding during the whole articulation process.....
so if you are one who is of a contrarian view to all that I've mentioned above, PLEASE by all means leave a comment or proceed to ignore my future posts. IT'S AFTER ALL, A FUCKING FREE WORLD (well, almost...)

30/10 (2) – AN UPDATED REPORT ON MY CURRENT PD CONDITION....

I would have to say that over this last year, the onslaught of the advancing effects of PD has been at its most brutal............the loss of my ability to articulate a coherent sentence being the second most devastating manifestation of this debilitating disease.

When i was first diagnosed about 5 1/2 years ago, i NEVER thought that I would lose the gift of speech....the kinds of rude and impatient responses from the ignorant who would just blurt out " can u speak slowly ah ? Not understand u lah !" & "cannot understand u, u pls speak to my colleague !" all this with the look of irritation and superiority on their faces.....this from Hotel receptionists, restaurant waiters, customer service execs, Bank managers and of course the FUCKING McDonald's call centre (minus the look), just to name a few.

The most distressing effect of PD on me however, has to be the frequent falls that i endure at a ridiculous frequency of twice a day (average) ! The number of times i had been admitted to hospital as a result of these falls would be laughable if not true...my knees, my palms, my wrists and elbows have now the appearance of deformity.

The 3rd on the list has to be the feeling of abject loss of energy, strength to get up or continue a movement from a stationery position. It is so wheelchair binding that it totally fucks up your mind.......

And as the kind but somewhat tactless GH Doctor said, things are going to get WORSE. Ohhh I can't fucking wait........

12/11 – REGRETS ?....TOO FEW TO MENTION. AND Y I DO(DID) THE THINGS I DO(DID)....

Life's a BITCH....u know y ? Becoz all i have to look forward to now on a daily basis is getting up in the mornings and falling on (not "to") my knees on exactly the same spots as the previous days. On a more recent note, I lost all feeling from the waist down about a week ago and I want to say is a big thank you to the security head at my condo who bundled me into a cab and sent me off to SUK Hospital. Needless to say, that episode left me with a big hole in my pocket (was in ICU) but with mixed feelings (a matter for another day)

So as the revelation that PD is surely well on its way to devouring me, its perhaps a good time to reflect on my life esp. the "Bangkok years", so that when i am no longer around, I hope that at least "one" of my dear readers will at least have (against the tide of Casual non-committers) understood and appreciated that i tried to lived the life that i had led, my way and on my terms (except the PD) and why I did the things I did...

To my readers who are happily married or have a distaste for anything sexual especially out of wedlock, I suggest you stop here.

As the post title says, I have very few regrets in my life, as I believe that I had endeavored to be the best dad, husband, son, brother and man that I could be, pre-PD diagnosis, and my closest buddies will attest to that, but something changed in JULY of 2011, something broke, something spoke and some things were just changing in ME that I just could not or would not comprehend.... b4 I proceed, my only 2 regrets in life:

1) That i broke my dad's heart by fucking up my "UK" years
2) That my son whom I dearly love has chosen to disown me.

TO BE CONTINUED....

13/11 -AN UNADULTERATED ACCOUNT OF MY BKK YEARS….

So, my son (& daughter) have both not spoken to me for over a half year now (in my daughter's case) since I made it a point to speak to them on a person to person level before I revealed my misdemeanors to my then wife.

My girl did not take the news well at all, that her father had fathered another child whilst in BKK with another woman and in spite of my attempts to explain myself, chose to walk out of the cafe we (her Polish BF was with us) were having bfast in, and so that episode together with a subsequent one a few days later, where i again tried to explain myself and where i got the same response, told me that here and now is where my little girl (now 27 years old) was my daughter no more. So, with that ended my relationship with my eldest child whom i had thought would understand the circumstances for all that had occurred in her father's life, this also taking into account the numerous occasions that she had told both my EX and i to go our separate ways…go figure…

A few months later, after i had sent a picture of her half-sister thru her BF'S fb message with the simplest words "pls forward this pic to K,,,,,,,a", I received this very nasty reply from her farang BF the contents of which revealed a guy (Jewish but minus the true traits and virtues of one) self-righteous and aloof whom i had thought better of….and so me being the type person who fucking hates when disrespected esp. by this young, caucasion know it all, gave him a piece of my mind to which there has been no response to-date…

TO BE CONTINUED…

14/11 – Continuation of "An unadulterated account of my BKK years"

My son was somewhat more tolerant, he at least made the effort to shout back this reply to me when we finally spoke to each other about 3 months back ;

"I am still very angry with you, I still love you, but what you did and the timing, was all wrong. I know we (sis & him) told you guys to go your separate ways but still….why didn't you just divorce mum first and then get remarried ? I would have stood by u all the way…..now I'm just still so upset…pls give me time, i can't say how long but…."

And with that ended my last communication with my son……my subsequent attempts to call, sms, whatsapp, viber or LINE him have met with silence.

So, why ? Why did I do what i did…..?

TO BE CONTINUED

21/11 – Y I DID THE SHIT I DID....

This is NOT an exercise in blame or hatred or revenge.

I loved my EX immensely. more than she ever could imagine (and that, as u will see, not for the last time, was due to ME) it's just the circumstances and the intense & immense change that i was unconsciously going thru on diagnosis of my PD till date. That is so absolutely brilliant to discover as I appreciate the feeling of non-stagnation in my growth as an individual and human being, for better or for worse..

I don't expect everyone to understand / appreciate / believe what I've gone thru' but it works as self- therapy to document whatever I can remember of my life before that too is taken from me......

TO BE CONTINUED....

22/11 – A SLIGHT DIGRESSION …

Perhaps a good time to reflect on my 3 years in BKK… To all my "peeps" who visited me over that period." thank you" for being my friends and i love u all… incl Effendy & Wilson & Peter Tait & Eric Neoh & Marciano & Subhas Datta whose pics i do not seem to have. Thanks for the memories !!!.

25/11 -Y I DID THE SHIT I DID...(II)

The author of "Parkinson's Disease Treatment – 10 Secrets to a Happier Life", Michael S Okun, said ;

'A person is defined by his Core Values and not by Parkinson's Disease.'

A tough target to achieve as the good doctor himself was diagnosed with PD when he was 60 and admitted that for 1 whole year following the diagnosis, he struggled to continue to live his life as normally as was possible.

Making the task doubly hard is trying to establish what your CORE VALUES are in the first place, for I am a firm believer that a person undergoes significant changes to his personality, character and behavior due to the forces exerted by circumstances or occurrences in his life, GOOD or BAD. Nevertheless, his book does lift my spirits and provide hope and that maybe I shouldn't be too quick to decide to "end it all" as I had done yesterday...

TO BE CONTINUED......

> The choice is yours to make,
> time is yours to take;
> some dive into the sea,
> some toil upon the stone.
>
> To live is to fly
> all low and high,
> so shake the dust off of your wings
> and the sleep out of your eyes.
>
> – Townes Van Zandt

25/11 (2) – Y I DID THE SHIT I DID...(III)

23/11 – morning, after making up my mind that i wanted to attempt a "JOB" driving for UBER back in Malaysia and having made the necessary inquiries to rent a condo at a strategic location, and having broken the news to my sister over whatsapp, the response I got from her was surprising to say the least. She went ballistic and started going on about how dangerous it would be for both me & the passenger(s), seeing as to how my PD condition had deteriorated to unprecedented levels....

However, me being the hard head that I am, I disagreed with her and insisted that I wanted to pursue my desire to be useful to my family & earn some extra money while I was still able to...I could still drive even though walking and standing upright without falling over had become insurmountable tasks of late. I would be sitting whilst in the car and hence the thought of falling would be non-existent. After all, on my trip back from Pattaya last month I had managed to hit a top speed of 20o km/hr whilst attempting to outrun a BMW on the Pattaya to Bangkok highway. So it was no big deal, so I thought. What happened next was a sure sign from God that my sister was castigating me for a reason, and that he had "elected" my sister to become my guardian angel and as sure as hell I had better listen to her, which he managed to convince me in a rather painful fashion...

TO BE CONTINUED..

6/12 – THE WHOLE FUCKING TRUTH AND NOTHING BUT...

AND, so as to send me a reminder that what i had in mind did not meet his approval, within the next five minutes (I fucking kid you not) he sent me tumbling to the ground so fast that i did not have time to attempt to break my fall and hit my head so hard on the fridge that i thought i would be concussed. I was so depressed after that incident that i told my wife that tonight i would end it all, so that she wouldn't interfere with my attempt like the last time but of course that did not work too...

So,

1. Because of these occurrences both physical and mental that PD has been bestowing me,

My ex and i met when i was 21 and she was 18 and it's a physical impossibility that persons of those ages would not grow and change with new people that they would meet or change with the circumstances that befell them. More so in the case of my Ex who was fresh out of school and much less so for me as i had spent 3 years in England before i had met her. And by the time i had met my current wife and had a child with her or rather by the time i had decided to embark on my PD crisis walk about in Bangkok, to say that my EX was a different animal from when we first met would be an understatement.

Now, that is not to say that i am BLAMING her for what happened, because the most shocking of changes to occur would be to me and that is due to Fucking PD (Please google PD & Sexual dysfunctions – Hyper sexuality)

TO BE CONTINUED

10/12 – MAP 2

As I started to tell Map that she had gotten my order wrong, her face turned even more red and fearful looking and that's when i muttered the words "it's ok, why don't I just take one portion and you can have the other portion with the other waitresses later and the last portion please give it to the lady boss seated at the cashier's counter." With those words, her face changed to one of relief, perhaps the thoughts of her salary being "cut" because of this error now having receded. Would I have done the same thing if the waitress concerned was a Fugly Young Thing instead ? Yes, if she'd shown genuine remorse as Map did...

So, with that episode over, I continued to enjoy the rest of the evening's rock & roll music and food and drinks until it was time to go home. That's when Map comes up to me and asked if I'd like to go to have coffee after she has cleaned up, to which I replied "sure"...

After about 15 mins of waiting, she comes out of the staff quarters, all happy and smiling and grabs my right arm and off we went to MCd's around the top of soi 4 where the old petrol station was and proceeded to chat till around 5 am and I asked where she lived and she mentioned "on nut, soi 20" to which I replied, "I know where that is as I live just on the opposite side of Sukhumvit soi 77"" (on nut) i.e. soi 50 and that we could take the same cab back. As the cab, pulls up to the entrance of her apartment, she suddenly turns to me and asks if I would like to spend the night with her, to which I replied in the affirmative...

TO BE CONTTINUED...

11/12 – AND NOW THE END IS NEAR...

As the award winning journalist and author of the book "Brain storms – The race to unlock the mysteries of Parkinson's Disease", Jon Palfreman mentions in his book, "the diagnosis marked an irreversible change in my identity, the moment that one version of me ended and another version began".

And that best describes how I felt then and how i feel now, and that with the "assistance" of L-Dopa and the Dopamine agonists had caused me to become that more disinhibited and that impulse control disorder had turned me into a sex addict...seeking out multiple relationships with different women, sometimes at the same time....

However I shall not go into the lurid accounts of each and every sexual encounter I had because I am mindful of my audience and so I shall just be concise in the descriptions of the acts and the persons involved (and on last count there were at least 1x0)...But seeing as to how important it has been to me to document everything as honestly as I can, there will be a more explicit version that I need to simultaneously log so that I can look back one day and remember the effects PD has had on my life. (If dementia hasn't set in yet). The one good news from all this shit that has happened is that I believe that with god's grace I have turned over a new leaf, after being caught in a threesome with 2 ladies neither of whom were my EX or current wives. The profound after effects of that episode just killed me...

TO BE CONTINUED